HOW TO HAVE A HAPPIER WIFE

Cecil G. Osborne

PYRANEE
BOOKS

Zondervan Publishing House
Grand Rapids, Michigan

How to Have a Happier Wife

This is a Pyranee Book
Published by the Zondervan Publishing House
1415 Lake Drive, S.E., Grand Rapids, Michigan 49506

This book is excerpted from *The Art of Understanding Your Mate*, copyright © 1970 by The Zondervan Corporation.

Library of Congress Cataloging in Publication Data

Osborne, Cecil G.
How to have a happier wife.

Excerpted from Osborne's The art of understanding your mate.
"Pyranee Books."
1. Husbands—Religious life. 2. Marriage—Religious aspects—Christianity. I. Osborne, Cecil G. Art of understanding your mate. II. Title.
BV4843.O72   1985   248.8'4   85-14255
ISBN 0-310-30622-1

Printed in the United States of America

87 88 89 90 / 10 9 8 7 6 5 4

Contents

1

Almost Any Marriage Can Be Improved

There is little less trouble in governing a
private family than a whole kingdom.
——*Montaigne*

There are undoubtedly some marriages which
were doomed from the start. There are individuals whose basic personalities are so fixed and
rigid, or whose behavior patterns are so neurotic, that is is difficult to imagine their achieving a satisfactory marriage relationship with
anyone.

But nearly all marriages can be improved,
and the vast majority of divorces could be
prevented by an appropriate course of counseling or group therapy. Those who expect marriage to solve their personality problems are
hopelessly unrealistic. In fact, marriage inten-
sifies neurotic tendencies.

5

One problem encountered in marriage is that of defining "spheres of influence." There are many variables, of course, but in a typical home the wife may have the final responsibility for the house, furniture, gardening, cooking, and the day-to-day responsibility of the children. In areas that represent the "nest" she will usually want to express her own taste in the furnishings of the home, but she will want her husband's approval. If he shows relative indifference, she perceives this as a rejection of her, since the home is an extension of her personality. If he is insistent upon making final decisions in matters pertaining to the selection of furniture or other details of the home, his wife will feel a loss of identity. She will become either hostile or frustrated. If she represses her anger, she may tend to become depressed.

A young couple, discussing their wedding plans with me, mentioned the fact that they had already selected their furniture. I asked how they arrived at the decision to purchase the particular style of furniture they had chosen. She was a gentle, quiet, nonassertive type of individual and deferred to him consistently. He, somewhat more aggressive, said, "Well, the kind of furniture she wanted would have been nice, but I held out for something more durable. We finally settled on a sturdy type that will stand up through the years." I asked her if she was happy with the selection. She insisted that it was quite acceptable to her, and I think it was—at that particular moment. She was deeply in love and had the instinctive feminine desire to please her husband.

But she will spend a great deal more time looking at that furniture than her practical husband will, and every time she dusts it she will remember that is was his choice, not hers. In time, whether she admits it to consciousness or not, she will detest the sturdy furniture that he picked out. She will take out her frustration on him, in either a direct or subtle manner, or if she is masochistic, she will turn her hostility inward and suffer from some physical or emotional symptom.

I said to them, "You will find greater happiness if you discover various 'spheres of influence.' For instance, if the wife can have the veto power around the house, and the husband can exercise his veto power in matters pertaining to his job, the car, and finances, you may have less conflict. These areas will vary from couple to couple, but we should avoid imposing our opinions on each other in too many areas."

A woman who is deprived of the right to exercise her own judgment in matters pertaining to her home can experience a definite loss of identity. It is not so important whether her taste or his is better. She should have the final say-so about the areas of the home which seem of vital importance to her. This may include the gardening, if she enjoys it. In one home the husband loved gardening, and his wife was only too happy to have him assume total responsibility for the yard. She rejoiced in his love of flowers, and she did not feel that this was an intrusion into her domain.

I have never particularly liked gardening. In fact, I despise it. But for some perverse reason, perhaps involving some subtle form of masochism, I kept at it for the first twenty years or so of marriage. One day I suddenly realized how utterly stupid it was of me to do the gardening when I hated every minute of it. I told my wife, "You're in charge of gardening hereafter. You can do it yourself, since you enjoy some aspects of it, or you can hire it done. I've just graduated. It is an extension of the house, and it's all yours."

And it has been so ever since. We did not arrive at the decision through lengthy discussion. It was a unilateral decision, but of course

I knew that she would not find it unacceptable. She was quite content to take over this added responsibility.

Earning a living is the fundamental responsibility of the husband, even though in our present culture millions of women work in order to supplement the family income, or because they desire some activity outside the home. When a married woman takes a job, it is often not an end in itself, but a means to an end. She may want to help pay off the mortgage, or save for the children's education, or buy some additional furniture.

Where the financial end of marriage is primarily, if not exclusively, a male responsibility, it is usually the husband who handles the finances. There are husbands who are good at it, and others who do a horrible job. I find wives who feel superior to their husbands in this regard and set up a rigid budget, allocating a precise amount for their husbands to spend for lunch, recreation, and personal expenses. One wife, who was actually more practical in the handling of money, came to see that her husband was feeling emasculated. He had tentatively suggested a number of times that he take back the checkbook, but his sloppy performance in the past caused her some hesitation. She asked, "Should I let him take it back?"

I said, "You sound like mother asking if she should let junior take out the family car. If he wants to try it again, why should he have to ask you? Are you playing the mother role and he the little-boy role?"

Rather hesitantly she handed him the checkbook a few days later and said, "I'm tired of this mess. Why don't you take it over?" She put the checkbook and the bills on his dresser. He took them rather casually and proceeded to do thereafter a creditable job, except that he would occasionally let some bills run two months or more.

His wife asked, "What shall I do if he keeps on letting bills go like that? It may ruin our credit."

"How will you ever find out if you don't keep your hands off and let him worry about it?" I replied. "If his education in this area has been neglected, he may as well learn how to go about becoming a responsible male. However, if the time ever comes when he makes a mess and actually wants you to take over this responsibility, and you do it at his request, that will be another matter."

In one home with several children there was

a certain amount of wrangling over whether disciplinary measures were too severe. In a typical incident, the mother had sent one of the teenage daughters to her room. The daughter appealed tearfully to her father, who she thought would support her. He said, "Honey, I think perhaps mother was a bit hard on you, but that's her ruling. You'll have to do as she says. There's nothing I intend doing about her decisions." A short time later mother cooled off and called the daughter to come down and join the family. All was serene.

Similarly, when the father issued some overly stern mandate, and the children appealed to the mother for sympathy and support, her response was that it was Daddy's ruling and they would have to work it out with him. This type of approach prevented the playing of one parent against the other. Sometimes a child will take advantage of an unresolved conflict between mother and father. If there is some smoldering resentment present, a child can appeal to one of the parents and get support, which in a sense is one parent's way of striking back at the other.

Basic Assumptions for Achieving Maturity

There are innumerable sources of conflict in a typical marriage, but the common denominator in working out a satisfactory relationship between the marriage partners is for both to seek spiritual and emotional maturity. In achieving this goal, there are certain basic assumptions which must be dealt with:

First, *no one person can satisfy all of our needs*. Each of us is a many-faceted person, and to expect some other individual to match each mood, satisfy every demand, and fulfill all of our needs is simply unrealistic. Every individual is different, and our needs differ from day to day and week to week. In addition, the inescapable differences of the sexes compound the problem.

Our basic human self-centeredness is responsible for the fact that we keep hoping that the marriage partner will perceive our emotional needs, perhaps by extrasensory perception, and unselfishly set out to meet them. The inner child, always in residence within us, waits expectantly for the perfect fulfillment of all our dreams.

The only possible approach to this innate egocentricity of ours is to apply literally the formula of Jesus: "Give, and it will be given unto you" (Luke 6:38). Instead of demanding, or expecting, that another will fulfill our needs, we must become mature enough to ask,

"How can I discover and satisfy the needs of my partner?" If some of them are unrealistic or selfish or childish, then at this point one can say, "This is a need of yours which I cannot, in all good conscience, fulfill." There need be no explosion (though such an explosion is not necessarily fatal).

The beautiful young wife of a struggling young husband had always dreamed of the home she would have someday. It would be spacious, filled with lovely furniture, and surrounded by a rolling lawn. Her adolescent dreams of entertaining in this beautiful home were all shattered when they moved into their first home—a tiny, cramped one-bedroom house. Her tears flowed for months. "This isn't the way I had thought it would be at all," she cried over and over. She turned her frustration and anger upon her husband. When I pointed out in a counseling session that her dreams could not be realized for some years, she vented her hostility upon me. One would have thought that the young husband and I had conspired to frustrate all of her dreams and aspirations. We had wrecked her doll house. It took three or four years for her to grow up emotionally and discover that her childish dreams could not be fulfilled by a magic wand or a marriage ceremony. In time she became a poised, emotionally mature young woman, accepting the realities of life, willing to abandon her unrealistic adolescent fantasies.

I had occasion to counsel with another young couple concerning some of their marital problems. In this instance the husband had never grown up completely. He had been reared in a home where nothing was demanded of him. He had never done any yard work or assumed any family responsibilities. It was not that he was selfish. It was simply that no one had ever required anything of him. Now the marriage was floundering, and we were able to trace many of their disagreements to the fact that Charles refused to do anything around the house. He had agreed to put some coat hangers in the hall closet months before, but had forgotten to. To a woman, neglect of the home is neglect of her as a person. The home is an extension of her own personality. His wife was outraged that he cared so little for her that he would not remember to put up the coat hangers.

His wife could easily have put them up, but she wanted him involved. Refusal to accept household responsibilities was evidence to her that he did not care about her. Gradually it

14

dawned upon Charles that he had been pampered as a child and that his responsibility as a husband involved more than earning a living.

The second basic assumption is that in the marriage relationship, *instead of waiting for our needs to be met, we must seek to meet the needs of the other.* The more emotionally mature we are, the fewer demands we make upon others, and the more capable we are of being concerned about others and their needs.

The proper question to ask is not, "How can I have all of my needs fulfilled in this marriage?" but "How much love can I express in meeting the needs of this person I married?"

Individuals differ in their needs. To one husband the way his shirts are ironed is a matter of major importance. To another this is trivial, but it is important to him that his wife not show up at the table in the clothes she wears when she mops the floors. One husband enjoyed his wife's extraordinarily fine cooking but never wanted to eat the same thing twice. Another man complained that his wife, who was an excellent cook, had such a mania for variety that he could never get her to cook the same dish twice. Still another husband was relatively indifferent to food and seldom knew what he was eating.

One husband feels a need to go into the kitchen and greet his wife affectionately when he returns from work, but his wife, harried with cooking and children, usually brushes him off with, "Oh, Henry, not now. Can't you see I'm busy?" She is trying to meet his needs by preparing an elaborate meal, when what he really wants more than a good meal is affection. She is giving him what she *thinks* he wants without being sensitive to his actual needs.

A perceptive wife, anxious to express love by meeting the needs of her husband, will try to discover whether she has grown up with some misconceptions about male needs. Just because her father was indifferent to whether meals were served on time does not mean that her husband is wired the same way. The needs of human beings vary enormously. It behooves a wife to become sensitive to her husband's needs and seek to meet them within the limits of her capabilities.

A wife has the primary responsibility for the "climate" in the home. This is true partly because women are more innately sensitive to persons and their needs, and partly because the home usually means more to the wife than it does to her husband. A woman has much more to gain from a good marriage and more to lose from a bad one. She may resent this fact, but it is still an inescapable fact of life. It therefore behooves her to make a career of trying to discover ways to please her husband. Women have a built-in need to please, to serve, to minister to the needs of others. Unless a woman is still immature and childish, she will want to discover ways of gratifying her husband's desires.

Along with this she has an equal need to be loved, cherished, and protected. She finds her security in feeling that her husband cares about her and is concerned for her welfare and happiness. In fact, at an unconscious level many women actually invent ways of discovering whether their husbands care deeply about them. Their deep insecurity requires constant reassurance.

A husband whose primary responsibility is to provide for the financial welfare of the family may come home from work with his physical and psychic energy depleted, to find that his wife has a list of things she wants to talk about. She may have accumulated a number of tasks for him to do around the house; or she is sick unto death of having children underfoot all day and wants to turn them over to him. Now they are in trouble! They have incompatible needs. She wants his help in taking care of the children, or she wants adult conversation; and he is too tired to be concerned for the moment about her needs. As man and woman they are basically incompatible in many areas to begin with, and now their momentary incompatibility has compounded this problem.

The general formula to be applied in this, or any similar impasse, is: don't expect too much of the persons around you, whether they be in-laws, children, or marriage partner. But if there are obvious things that you have a right to expect of others, the approach is all-important. A half-hostile, half-demanding manner is much less likely to get results than a gentle approach. A man is much more likely to yield to a gentle, seductive tone than to the "I'm fed up to here with these kids. You take over!" type of approach.

One young wife whose marriage was, as she put it, "coming apart at the seams," discussed her hostility over the fact that her husband never assumed any responsibility around the house. The facts that finally emerged were these:

He was worried about his job, which he felt

was threatened. He spent two hours a day commuting, eight hours on the job, and came home to brood about his worries, expecting affection and sympathy. As he put it, "She has one child and a small house to take care of. She can get out during the day and visit her friends when she wants to, or go shopping, and maybe squeeze in an hour or so of television if she feels like it. I have my nose to the grindstone eight full hours a day. I resent entering the door and being met with a barrage of complaints."

She countered with the complaint that he came home grumpy, seldom discussed anything with her, and refused any responsibility around the home. In reaction, she had become nervous and emotionally distraught. She could express no affection of any sort, for she felt unloved and neglected. Partly to escape from her complaints he was taking weekend fishing trips, which caused her to feel still more neglected.

Not because she was any more to blame than he, but because she was more susceptible to change, I met with her weekly for several months. We agreed on a number of things she could do to improve their marriage. I assured her that if she would take these steps, he would respond as soon as he found that she had actually changed.

She began to meet him at the door with a kiss instead of complaints. Instead of making demands or requiring an explanation as to where he went when he was away, she accepted him as he was. Rather than using tears to manipulate him, she began asking him what she could do to make him happy. She was an eager, intelligent young woman, and not once in our counseling did she ever resort to the "Yes, but—" habit. Within a few short months they had worked out a delightful marriage relationship. It was possible because the wife was willing to accept sole responsibility for initiating some changes in her own personality. Women are less obtuse in many ways and thus better equipped to initiate changes in the marriage relationship.

But men have responsibilities for the marriage, too. If the wife must more often take the initiative in improving the marriage, the husband bears an equal responsibility in responding to change in his wife's altered approach.

A typical wife with the usual number of standard complaints about an unresponsive husband joined a group of eight persons who were seeking solutions to various kinds of problems. She was told upon entering the group that we did not confess the faults of others. We were to share only our own deficiencies. She reported at one group session that her husband had said one evening after she returned home:

"Well, I suppose you gave them all the details about what a rotten husband I am."

She said, "No, on the contrary, we're not allowed to confess the sins of others. We just talk about what we can do to improve ourselves."

He made no comment. A few months later, when it became obvious to him that she was making a valiant attempt to correct some of her own faults, he said, "I suppose you'll be wanting me to join one of those groups."

She said, "No, that isn't my responsibility."

"You mean you don't want me in the group?"

"Oh, I suppose you could join a group if you wanted to, but it's purely voluntary."

A month or so later he said, "I might just visit one of these stupid groups and see what goes on."

"No, they won't permit visitors. You have to join for at least three months."

"Are there other husbands in some of the groups?"

"Yes, quite a number."

"Whom do I talk to about joining a group?"

She told him, and rather hesitantly he asked to join a group. Before the first session was over, he was participating freely. At the end, he said, "I had actually intended to make this a one-night stand, but I've enjoyed it. There ought to be more places where people can be themselves and learn how to be honest. I'm going to keep coming."

In a group session a woman quoted, in a facetious vein: "He took it like a man—he blamed it on his wife." There is an almost universal tendency to blame someone else for our problems. It began in the Garden of Eden when God asked Adam about eating the forbidden fruit. Adam said, "The woman . . . gave me the fruit of the tree, and I ate." Eve, unwilling to accept her guilt, said, "The serpent beguiled me" (Genesis 3:12–13). Perhaps if the serpent could have been queried, he might have said, "My environment made me this way." Most of us are born buck-passers. We begin to achieve a measure of maturity only when we cease to blame others and accept the responsibility for change within ourselves.

There is a spiritual that expresses a great truth:

'Tain't my brother nor my sister,
But it's me, O Lord;
Standing in the need of prayer.

Emotional Barriers to Communication

The basic physical and emotional differences between men and women are great. Future generations may well read with astonishment that young people were once permitted to marry without a year or two of intensive study of the complexities involved in this, the most important of all human relationships. A man, for instance, can never know what it feels like to be pregnant, to nurse a baby, or to experience the up-and-down moods that accompany the feminine cycle. No man can fully comprehend how a woman's inner calendar affects her moods and her consequent responses to him. Women in general rate higher on "nurturing," the desire to provide loving care for others. Men are generally more competitive and aggressive; even if they are not innately so, our culture tends to fit them into this mold. Men are usually less able to express their feelings and are often unaware of some of their deeper emotions. Consequently they can be uncomprehending or impatient with the more volatile emotions of their wives.

Neither sex fully understands the other. We view each other through a lattice of our own physical and emotional responses, expecting our varying emotional needs to be understood and met even though we may not be able to express them.

It is precisely at this point that communication becomes so vitally important. Communication is not "just talking." It involves the willingness and capacity to express our feelings to each other. Such feelings may not always be positive. Often they will be negative, involving anger or hurt or disappointment.

A common barrier to communication between husband and wife is the instinctive tendency to blame and attack. In a group session in which a husband and wife participated, the wife expressed dissatisfaction with her husband's inability to communicate. "He comes home, reads the paper until dinner time, gulps his food, then plants himself in front of the television set. He never takes me anywhere, never reads a book, never talks to me."

Her husband was showing signs of growing tension, which he sought to control. He was playing the strong, silent, uncomplaining role for the moment. He forced a grin, as his wife finished her tirade. "Yeah, that's the kind of bum I am, I guess. I never was much for talking. I'm tired at night, and I suppose I'm not a very good husband."

One of the men said, "Hank, you make me tired. Your wife has done nine-tenths of the talking since you two joined the group. She has berated you, downgraded you, condemned you on a dozen counts, and you just sit there absorbing all this punishment as though you deserved it. Maybe you do, in part, but you can't be the hopeless person she makes you out to be. Why don't you defend yourself? Wouldn't your mother ever let you talk back? Were you terrified of your mother, and now of your wife? For heaven's sake, stand up to this woman! She has a grievance, but you must have some of your own!"

Hank looked thoughtful. "You mentioned my mother. She was a pretty stern person, but she loved us all. I can't recall ever getting mad, or at least I never showed it. It wasn't allowed at our house. Mom and Dad didn't talk much between themselves, and I guess I just became a silent person in order to stay out of trouble. I've never had a verbal battle with anyone in my life, and I don't feel disposed to start at this late date. My wife will either have to get used to my silence or get another husband, I guess." He paused and looked grim for a moment. "And I just now realized for the first time that I don't care much which she does. I've about had it."

The group leader interrupted at this point and said, "I think we'll go into a role play session, with Hank as the husband and Marian as the wife. Marian, the setting is this: Hank is your 'role play' husband. He is silent, uncommunicative, out of touch with his feelings. You feel neglected and lonely. You've tried everything in the way of verbal taunts and abuse to no avail. Just now you've discovered that Hank has planned a three-day hunting trip with a friend, and you have decided to try to let him know how you feel about this. Remember, you cannot change Hank by direct action or by manipulation, but you have a right to let him know how you feel."

Hank and Marian sat facing each other in the center of the circle, while Hank's wife looked on with a mixture of emotions. Marian began gently:

"Hank, could I talk with you for a few minutes?"

"Sure, why not?"

"Well, Hank, I've been thinking lately about what a nag I've become. About all I've said to you in the last year or two has been either petulant or nagging. And I don't want to go on being this kind of a person. I hate myself when I do this."

"Yeah? What brought you to this conclusion?"

"Oh, I just got to listening to myself. Don't you agree that I've been sounding pretty much like a fishwife lately?"

"Yes, sort of."

"I suppose it's because in the home where I grew up everyone talked all the time, and I guess I imagined all families would be like that—talking things over, arguing, loving, fighting." She paused.

Hank said, "My father and mother didn't talk much to each other, except to yell. I hate yelling. I remember always going to my room when Mom and Dad argued."

"You retreated?"

"Yeah. I guess I still do, especially when you start sounding hostile."

"You've never told me about your family before, how hostile they were."

"You've never asked me."

"You're right. I suppose I brought to mar-

27

riage some preconceived notions about how it would be. We'd sit and hold hands and talk, and share . . . and when it didn't work out that way, I started feeling lonely, then rejected, and then abused."

"I'm sorry. I'm just not much of a talker. Maybe you married the wrong guy."

"No, I don't think so. I just made a mistake in imagining that all men would be like my dad; but you have a lot of traits I admire or I wouldn't have married you."

"So?"

"Look, Hank, I've been all wrong in trying to change you. I've criticized you and attacked you, and your natural response has been to retreat; I'm responsible. At least I'm responsible for attacking you."

"And I guess I'm responsible for the way I react. Maybe I could learn to be more communicative, but I just can't react with affection when you're hostile."

"Look, Hank, I want to stop trying to change you. You just be yourself, and I'll stop criticizing you. I do love you, and I don't want to drive you out of the house or into your silent self with my attacks?"

"You don't drive me out of the house. I go of my own free will."

28

"Couldn't this hunting trip be partly an effort to escape from my tirades?"

Hank was silent for a long minute. "Maybe so. I just feel more at peace when I'm out in the woods with a friend. He and I don't criticize each other."

"Hank, I want you to know that after this I'll never complain when you go hunting, or anywhere else for that matter. I do feel lonely, I'll admit. I'd like to be with you and go places with you; but maybe I'm not very good company, the way I've been acting."

She reached out and took Hank's hand. He smiled. He was a passive male who had been retreating from a demanding, hostile, aggrieved wife. Marian's tenderness reached into some hidden recess of his soul, and he responded. He was no longer playing a role. He squeezed her hand.

"Honey, I don't think I'll go on that hunting trip. I'd rather stay here with you. Perhaps we could do something . . . maybe dinner and a show?"

"I'd love that." Marian got up and kissed him tenderly on the cheek. Hank stood up and hugged her.

Hank and Marian resumed their seats in the circle. Hank's wife was weeping silently.

When she had regained her composure, she said, "I saw myself for the first time for the nagging, demanding wife I am, and hate myself for it. I saw Hank melt when he was confronted with an understanding wife. I have been battering him, not loving him. I have been confessing his faults, instead of my own. I've done it all backward."

Hank walked over to her and said, "Honey, I'm an uncommunicative slob. I don't think I've tried very hard to overcome my lifelong hangup about talking. But I think I can do better. I see that it's not a passion for hunting, but an effort to escape from having to communicate or face your anger."

"Hank," she said. "I talk faster and more than you, but I can see now that I'm no better at communicating than you. Suppose we keep on trying, at home and in this group, to learn more about real communication."

They did not become proficient overnight, but in time they both learned to express their deeper feelings. There were moments of hurt and hostility, but they rode over these and learned that even anger can be creative at times. He learned to face and express his feelings, and she discovered that love and patience work miracles.

"Coded Messages"

Most married couples send "coded messages" quite unconsciously. They hope the other will decode the message and give an appropriate reply. Here is a typical series of coded messages, with their real meanings in parentheses:

Wife: "I've had a terrible day. The kids were perfectly awful, and I've got a splitting headache." (I'd like for you to put your arms around me and tell me you love me and that you understand how rough I have it; and maybe you could take us all out to a drive-in for dinner.)

Husband: "You've had a terrible day! Wait 'til you hear what happened to me. There was an accident on the freeway, and I was a half-hour late to work. The boss bawled me out and wouldn't let me explain. Then my secretary was home sick, and I had a whole mess of correspondence that had to go out. On top of that I goofed up a sales contact and the sales manager gave me a bad time. Good grief. What a day!" (You can stay home and watch television if you feel like it, or visit with your friends, or go shopping, while I knock myself out trying to earn a living for this family. What

I need is some peace and quiet while I pull myself together. Maybe a little understanding would help, too, and all I hear is complaints. What do you *do* all day?)

Wife: "Honey, will you take these kids off my hands and get them out of the kitchen while I try to get some dinner on the table?" (I've had these kids all day, and I deserve a little peace. You never really do anything with our kids. You're not a very good father, to tell the truth.)

Husband: "Sure, sure. Kids, all of you get out of the kitchen. Go clean up the living room and wash up for dinner." (What a mess this house is! It looks like a cyclone hit it. Why can't you keep this place picked up a little or teach the kids some responsibility? Where can I go to get away from all this racket, and pull myself together?)

At dinner:
Wife: "The washing machine broke down today. Would you take a look at it after dinner?" (It would give a feeling of security or something if you'd take a little interest in what goes on around this house.)

Husband: "Yeah. I'll look at it, but I doubt if I can fix it. Those things are pretty complicated." (Why can't you call the repairman? I'm not a mechanic. I need some rest after a hectic day, and I come home to a bunch of screaming kids and a broken washing machine. I have no intention of spending the evening sitting on the floor looking at the insides of a busted appliance I don't know a thing about.)

After dinner:

Wife: "Jimmy's teacher called today. She says he's a disruptive element in the class and shows signs of emotional disturbance. She thinks one of us ought to go and talk to her about it." (I want some help in raising this brood. If you'd just take a serious interest in these things, I'd feel much better. In fact if you'd just give me some undivided attention while I talk about it instead of sneaking looks at that newspaper, I'd feel that you really care about us.)

Husband: "Okay. Maybe you'd better drop in and see his teacher tomorrow. I'll talk to Jimmy in a day or so and tell him to shape up. He's really getting out of hand. But I guess it isn't too serious. My teachers were always sending notes home about me when I was his age." (Why can't you handle a little session with the kid's teacher? One would think this was a major catastrophe. I handle fifty issues a day more important than this. Why are women so helpless? I wish I could read the evening paper without all of this rehash of the day's minor issues.)

At breakfast:

Wife: "Oh, dear, I forgot to tell you mother is coming to visit us for a few days. You'll have to clear your fishing gear out of the guest room. She's coming this afternoon. Could you do it before you leave for the office?" (I hated to tell you this while you were tired last night. For some reason you have this unreasonable hostility toward my mother. I know she can be a little difficult and overtalkative at times, but after all, she is my mother. I hope you'll be nicer to her than you were the last time she was here.)

Husband: "Oh? She's coming this afternoon? Well, I guess it won't be too terrible if I'm late two days in a row. I'll skip the rest of my breakfast and get that fishing gear stowed away." (Old Vesuvius is coming again! The last time she came for a few weeks, she stayed three months, and by the time she left, the kids were out of control and all of us were at each other's throats. Why must she descend on us

34

and wreck what little peace we have? She's always resented me, and frankly I can't stand having her around. She takes over the house, spoils the kids, and runs things to suit herself. She treats us all as if we were idiots incapable of handling our own lives. I'll try to be polite, but it isn't going to be easy. You don't like her visits any better than I do, but you're too loyal to dear old Mom to admit it, even to yourself!)

And so it goes. In millions of homes the coded messages are sent back and forth day after day, year after year, while the tensions silently mount until, when some minor issue arises, one or the other explodes in what would seem to be a senseless display of anger. The explosion, whether taking the form of muffled underground rumbling, or of silent withdrawal, can usually be attributed to the daily accumulation of unresolved irritations because they were unexpressed and thus unresolved.

What Are the Alternatives?

The alternatives would seem to be, at first glance, to keep on sending polite coded messages or to talk the problem out explosively. The first alternative involves temporary peace at the price of slowly accumulating hostility. The second choice, speaking one's mind honestly and freely, all too often results in wounded feelings and failure to resolve the basic difficulty. "Speaking the truth in love," is generally a better solution than blurting out the honest and hurtful truth. To be loving is more important than to be honest, yet to be loving involves facing, at times, the fact that one must speak honestly.

There are times when true feelings must be shared, provided that the marriage partner is able to face and accept the truth. We have no moral right to unload all our hostile feelings on another who may be emotionally unequipped to deal with that much anger.

In small groups in the past few years, several thousand husbands and wives have worked through, and resolved, basic marital problems. Yokefellow groups, as they are called, are not solely "therapy groups," yet this is often one vital aspect of their activity. It is usually easier to work through a difficult marital problem in a small sharing group than it is at home. Very often husbands and wives learn for the first time how to communicate within the circle of a group of people with similar problems. The group does not seek so much to deal with the symptom, but to find the basic cause of the problem.

A seriously depressed wife came to me for counseling. She had always been a happy person, she said, until the past year. Gradually she had become depressed and unhappy, yet there was nothing significant in her story to account for her morbid depression. The children were not too happy in their new home, and her husband appeared to be somewhat rigid, but none of this seemed sufficient to explain her mental condition. After a number of private sessions, I suggested that we might get to the root of the problem more readily if she and her husband would join a group. He came with her to the first meeting with serious reservations. He proved to be a quiet, somewhat reticent person. As he said later, he had no intention of washing his dirty linen in public, but he had agreed to come to "see what is was all about," and because his wife urged him to do so.

There was no single problem to resolve. He discovered that he was much out of touch with his emotions and became exceedingly angry over seeming trifles. He was basically compliant and agreed to his wife's suggestions, though often with buried hostility. She feared his angry outbursts, whether directed at her or a neighbor, and had begun to withdraw. As the result of burying her true feelings, she turned her resentment inward upon herself, and depression was the result.

They shared nothing sordid or intimate, yet each seemed able to express real feelings in the group more readily than at home. There was a certain safety in the group. Others had similar or identical problems. The atmosphere of total acceptance made it easier to be honest and open.

Within a relatively short time both husband and wife reported significant dividends. He said, "I find myself able to function better at work, with less hostility toward fellow workers. I am not so irritable, either at work or at home. I guess I was a very hostile person, and didn't realize it. I'm learning how to handle my anger in a more creative way."

She said, "My depression has diminished greatly, now that I'm able to say, in the group, what I feel. At home I often feared to say what I felt for fear I would hurt my husband's feelings, or because he might become angry. The children must have picked up some of my depression, and perhaps some of his hostility, because they were out of focus. They are now reacting differently, probably because *we* are different."

I have no desire to oversimplify the matter of communication or to suggest that a few months in such a group always will quickly resolve difficult problems of long standing. But it can happen.

2

Ten Commandments for Husbands

Here are ten commandments for husbands:

    I. Treat your wife with strength and gentleness.

  II. Give ample praise and reassurance.

 III. Define the areas of responsibility.

 IV. Avoid criticism.

   V. Remember the importance of "little things."

 VI. Recognize her need for togetherness.

VII. Give her a sense of security.

VIII. Recognize the validity of her moods.

 IX. Cooperate with her in every effort to improve your marriage.

  X. Discover her particular, individual needs and try to meet them.

I. Treat Your Wife With Strength and Gentleness

No matter how self-reliant a woman may be, regardless of her intelligence, capability, and drive, even if she seems dominant, there is something within her which wants to "lean" on a man. Reduced to its basic elements, a woman wants to be "taken, and taken care of." She wants to feel that she has been chosen (even if she has actually done the initial choosing). She would like to be swept off her feet, and then taken care of with gentleness and strength.

These two qualities are basic. Your wife may discover that you are not always as strong as she had hoped, nor as perfect, and sometimes perhaps not as gentle. If she married you taking your passivity for gentleness and your quietness for strength, she will be disappointed.

In a group session a wife was complaining about her husband's passivity. She said, "He is very gentle and quiet—too quiet. He never has any ideas of his own. I make most of the decisions. I can have my way about almost anything. I don't *want* my way all the time. I want him to take the lead, to initiate and plan.

I even plan our vacations. He lets me do about anything I want. I just wish he'd put his foot down once in a while and tell me I *couldn't* do something."

"Suppose you knew you were right," I said, "and he stubbornly put his foot down and insisted on having it done his way. Would you go for that?"

"I'd enjoy that," she replied. "I'm sick and tired of making all the decisions."

"But if he did start making decisions, you'd put up an argument, wouldn't you?"

"Sure, almost any woman would. But I don't really want to win. I want him to win part of the time. I want him to be stronger than I am."

"But you picked out a passive male," I said. "Something in you sensed his passivity, you wanted it, and now you are complaining."

She was thoughtful. "Well, I guess the human part of me wanted someone I could manage and control, but the feminine part of me wants a man who is strong enough to make me behave—even when I put up a fuss."

This confusing ambivalence on the part of a woman can be irritating or infuriating to a man who sees it as illogical. You, as a husband, might feel like saying to such a wife, "Look! If you want me to be in charge, stop putting up a battle over every issue. After knocking myself out at work, I don't want to have to come home and spend what little psychic energy I have left fighting a mock battle over some trivial issue. Maintain your identity in some other way, but don't give me an argument over each issue that arises." Even such a speech as that could, in a sense, indicate to your wife that you *are* taking charge.

Being in charge does not mean being "the boss" or becoming domineering. Only a very insecure man feels a need to force his will on others. Strength does not imply throwing your weight around, issuing orders, and demanding obedience of everyone within earshot.

This combination of strength and tenderness is not easily achieved if one does not possess it innately, but you can work at it. You may make mistakes, but with patience and determination you can satisfy your wife's inner need for emotional security with a quiet strength that is gentle and tender.

II. Give Ample Praise and Reassurance

For thousands of years women were in a subordinate position. Only in this century have they achieved equality in voting and property rights and partial equality on the job.

Their rights are newly won, and the ancient insecurities are still resident in the female emotional structure.

In addition, the role of mother renders the woman much more vulnerable and insecure. Instinctively she feels a need for someone to protect her and her children and to provide for the family. This generates a kind of all-pervasive insecurity which exists whether there are children or not, or after the children have left the nest. Some women are extremely reluctant to reveal to a man the extent of their insecurity and their desperate need for a husband to "lean" on. But it is there.

Because of this and other factors, women need considerable reassurance. It can be given in the form of praise, recognition, or commendation, or simply by saying, "I love you!" — often. When a woman asks, "Do you love me?" she isn't asking for information. She is asking for reassurance.

One husband, who found it extremely difficult to express tenderness verbally, complained that his wife was always asking if he loved her.

"Of course I love her. She ought to know that! I bring home my paycheck and hand it over to her. I take care of her and the kids. If I didn't love her, would I be hanging around? The boss doesn't tell me every day what a fine job I'm doing. In fact, no one has complimented me on my work in twenty years, but I am pretty sure of a job. Why do women need all of this sentimental stuff?"

"That's the way they are," I said. "Women are simply made that way and you had better accept it as a fact. Since verbal expression of affection is a need of hers, go along with it whether you feel like it or not."

"But that would be hypocritical if I didn't happen to feel like it at the moment."

"Not at all," I replied. "It is never hypocritical to do the appropriate thing. In time you will discover that your feelings will catch up with your actions, and you won't feel so clumsy in expressing tenderness." He agreed to try.

III. Define the Areas of Responsibility

In a relationship between any two persons, there must be a tacit understanding of the areas of responsibility. If two men are in partnership, they must work out the spheres of activity and have them clearly defined. The same thing holds with equal force in a marriage relationship.

Some areas seem clearly enough defined. Your wife takes care of the house, cooks, and has the primary responsibility for the children, particularly when they are very young. You earn the living. But there are many other less clearly defined areas.

Who takes out the garbage? Who is responsible for the lawn, choosing the new car, deciding where to spend the vacation? Who has the veto power on making investments or where to live? Who is primarily responsible for seeing the teacher when one of the children is having difficulty at school? Who decides when to buy a new washing machine or new furniture? Who casts the deciding vote concerning what to do on weekends—whether time will be spent with the children, with friends, or on some hobby?

A simplistic answer is: "Let the final decision rest with the one who is best qualified." Unfortunately this is a gross oversimplification. You, as husband, could easily abdicate responsibility by saying, "Look dear, you're a lot better at that than I am. Why don't you just take care of it and not bother me with details?"

There is, to the male, a "peculiarity" of the feminine nature which, in most cases, wants the husband to participate. A wife often feels more "secure" if she can talk things over with her husband. She may choose a time to do this when you want to read, play golf, or watch television. You can become grossly irritated over what may seem to you to be minor issues. But life consists not only of major decisions. Marriage is mostly "little things," which to a male can be an excruciating bore. But this is a part of marriage and of living.

A couple must find out for themselves where the various "spheres of influence" lie: who pays the bills, who casts the deciding vote on buying what house, renting which apartment, where to vacation. A selfish husband or wife may insist on rendering a final verdict on all decisions, major and minor; but marriage involves *resolving the incompatible needs of two different people.*

Generally, a wife's decision about the house or apartment, the furniture, and details pertaining to the "nest" should be given priority. As a man's job is an extension of his personality, the home is an extension of the wife's even if she is employed outside the home. Her job, if she works, is often only a means to an end, not a major part of her life.

"We'll decide these things together," a young couple told me as we discussed their forthcoming marriage. At that point they could not even begin to envision the countless decisions concerning which they would have divergent views and needs. When there is a difference of opinion, the couple must decide whether this matter falls within his sphere or hers, and whether he or she has the veto power.

A husband who bought eight cars in five years exasperated his wife with his total disregard for the realities of their budget. She brought it up in a group session. She was extremely conservative concerning money, and he had no concept of how to live within a budget. They were always heavily in debt. His immaturity in the handling of money and in other areas had resulted in a separation. Now they were in a group trying to effect a reconciliation. Over a period of months he came to perceive that he had been acting in an immature fashion in certain areas, and said, "I'm a whiz at my job. I earn plenty of money, but I'm not very good at handling it. I'd like for Marie to take over the handling of our finances."

I asked, "Will this make you feel like a little boy, with 'Mother' allotting you so much to spend each week?"

"Not at all, at this point. It would have a year

ago. I think I've matured enough to let her handle the finances." His wife was not a controlling type of person and in this instance the plan worked well.

IV. Avoid Criticism

A woman tends to lose her identity somewhat more readily than a man, other things being equal. A man who constantly criticizes and condemns his wife can produce numerous negative results in his wife. She may:

- Become deeply depressed through repressing her hostility
- Develop one or more physical symptoms, since the mind tends to hand its pain over to the body
- Become hostile, emotionally unresponsive, or sexually frigid
- Lose her identity through being constantly beaten down
- Unload her resentment onto the children and cause emotional disturbances in them
- Decide to give up the marriage

A regular barrage of criticism, even when warranted, is always destructive. In fact, almost all criticism is destructive. There is usually a better way to achieve results.

A woman who liked to read a great deal and

had numerous outside activities, admitted in her group session that she was a poor housekeeper. Her husband complained from time to time about it. Finally he said, "My criticism of her housekeeping is getting us nowhere. I don't know what her block is. I'm not a perfectionist, but I would like to see the house halfway cleaned at least once a week. I'm embarrassed to have a house that looks like ours, and to have a wife who does such a sloppy job. I'm going to stop carping about it. But I have the same right to a decent house as she has to expect me to earn a decent living. I'm going to decide on some positive solution. Give me a week to think it out."

The next week he had his answer. "I told her quietly and without hostility that if she had a block about housekeeping, I'd handle my job and clean up the house too until she overcame her neurotic block. This week I have come home from work and started doing housework. I am trying not to play the martyr, though I do admit I'm not overly happy about this solution. I am going to do this until she gets sick of abdicating her responsibility. If it takes six months or ten years, I will do my job and hers, without comment. I know she has either a neurotic block or a total incapacity to keep house. When she gets tired of goofing off, or sick of her neurosis, she can take over the housekeeping."

This was said with some impatience, but also with a considerable measure of understanding. In their particular case, the procedure worked. She did have an emotional block. Her mother had been a fanatically meticulous housekeeper, and at an unconscious level she had resolved to be as unlike her mother as possible. She worked this block out in her group, and in a matter of months began to assume her household duties. When she slipped back into her old ways, as she did at times, her husband quietly took over again. In time she was able to function normally as a housekeeper.

Criticism in any area is inevitable in almost any human relationship, but the less there is, the more satisfactory the marriage will be. This does not rule out expressing one's feelings. There are, however, different ways of saying the same thing:

"Do you realize we have just about the same kind of meal day in and day out? Why can't you get some kind of variety into our meals?"

Or, "You know, dear, you're a good cook, and I enjoy your meals, but when I was a kid we had the same kind of food week in and week out. Mom wasn't a very good cook, and I resolved that when I got married, I'd have some variety in my meals. There's nothing wrong with this food, but I'd prefer a little variety. Just one of my idiosyncrasies."

"Can't you keep these kids quiet? Look, when I come home from work I deserve a little peace and quiet."

Or, "Honey, I've had a hard day, and I know you've had a rough time with the kids, too. They must get on your nerves. I expect you'd like to turn them over to someone else and get a little relief. Unfortunately I just haven't got much steam left when I get home. Tell you what: I'll try to get the kids under control when I come home, while you get dinner; and after dinner I'll go pull myself together for a bit. Then we can sit down and have a little time to ourselves. Okay?"

These are not suggested as "solutions," but simply as different ways of saying the same thing. Just because we are married we do not have the right to be insulting or tactless and critical. The marriage license is not a license to insult.

V. Remember the Importance of "Little Things"

Men are usually less sentimental than women and attach less importance to such things as birthdays, anniversaries, "little" gestures that mean much to women. Love is not just a feeling; it involves positive actions which can mean a great deal to a woman.

I have long been aware of the principle, but like a typical male, I had not let it filter down into the feeling level of my nature. I once asked my wife what she wanted for Christmas. Although, like any woman, she likes surprises, I felt that there was nothing I could get her in the nature of a surprise which would fill any particular need. She surprised me by saying that all she wanted for Christmas was to have a large tree cut down just outside our bedroom window. She had mentioned this numerous times, but I had delayed because of the considerable expense involved. I agreed and long before Christmas I found an opportunity to have the tree removed. Then Christmas arrived, and I felt a need to put something under the tree for her. Her physical needs and wants were, so far as I could see, well supplied. She could think of nothing she particularly wanted.

Christmas Eve came, and I still had no idea what I could get her. Sitting at my desk I began, rather halfheartedly, to work on a crazy-to-me little idea. I cut out a dozen three by five sheets of paper and stapled them together with a cover to form a coupon book.

On one I wrote: Good for One Dinner at a First-Class San Francisco Restaurant. The second one read: Good for One Dinner at a Drive-In with Entertainment Afterward. The third was for One Dinner at a Medium-Priced Restaurant. The fourth was good for a dinner at a Chinese Restaurant. Another coupon entitled her to a meal at a steak house. One was for a dinner "at a first-class restaurant, to be earned by meritorious conduct beyond the call of duty," and so on. There were twelve in all, to be used at her discretion.

I felt rather sheepish about the whole deal. It was a crude little coupon book and involved only some dinners and fun which she had every right to expect anyway. To my surprise she was thrilled, because she could pull out a coupon on any free night I might have (rare enough in my case) and decide where we would go for dinner. Eating out in a restaurant is no great treat for me, and I knew this was not true for her, but I was not prepared for the great satisfaction it gave her to know that I was setting aside twelve evenings for dining out.

Men are nearly always surprised to discover how much "little things" (as they deem them to be) mean to a woman—an unexpected gift, a compliment on a new dress, or a sincere, "You look great with the new hairdo, Honey."

A husband who forgets a wedding anniversary has committed an almost unforgivable sin. Mother's Day, Easter, and Christmas all call for recognition. A young wife married to an unresponsive husband told me that she felt cheated by his lack of consideration of her needs. Part of her resentment was passed on to him in the form of criticism, and part to the children when he wasn't around.

Finally, realizing that direct criticism was useless and destructive, she sat down with him and explained her needs as a woman. She asked him gently to recognize her emotional needs. He just grunted and said he would think about it. But a week or two later he brought her an unexpected gift with a tender expression of love. He had not been unwilling, just uncomprehending. Her former tirades had evoked only hostility or silence. The quiet expression of her needs helped him understand for the first time and enabled him to respond.

"I don't want to have to remind my husband of our anniversaries," one wife said. "That takes all the fun out of it; and I don't want to have to make all the suggestions about going out, or to dinner. I'd love it if just once he'd initiate something, take the lead, show me that he cares, plan something for us without asking me." This is a legitimate female need, and a husband must recognize it if he is to be an adequate marriage partner.

VI. Recognize Her Need for Togetherness

No two women are identical in their needs, of course, but in general women tend more often than men to require a sense of "togetherness." This term is much overworked, but the truth it involves cannot be ignored. There is the dependent, possessive, clinging, demanding wife who doesn't want her husband out of her sight. She is in need of counseling, for her neurotic needs spring out of a deep insecurity, but even a typical wife may often want more of her husband's time and attention than he feels like giving her.

Many husbands enjoy family outings. Some men enjoy all manner of activities with their wives, while others have a strong need for male companionship. A husband who wants to preserve a good marriage relationship will try to meet his wife's need for doing things together. If their recreational tastes differ, then a compromise is indicated.

I recall a summer when my wife expressed a desire to spend our vacation at a summer resort. I felt an urge to take a pack trip with some men. She detested camping, and I had no particular desire to sit around a resort with no opportunity for fishing. After a brief discussion, we arranged a compromise. We had two weeks to spend, so I suggested that I would spend one week with her at the resort and one week on a pack trip into the mountains where I could get in some fly fishing. She agreed readily. It was an altogether satisfactory arrangement. She did not in the least mind being left alone for a week because she made friends readily.

A clinging, demanding, possessive wife could make such an arrangement difficult if not impossible. Virtually all husbands and wives have some incompatible needs. Togetherness does not imply that we will go through life hand in hand, always enjoying identical things to the same degree. We are still individual humans with divergent needs and tastes. We must respect the needs of others and compromise cheerfully when necessary. Only the immature and childish demand to have their way under all circumstances.

VII. Give Her a Sense of Security

A woman's need for security is much greater than most men imagine. It can be provided by a husband who is strong, gentle, and considerate. But in specific areas women's needs vary. Many women derive a sense of security (often without being aware of it) from having a husband who does household repairs. This means that he is interested in the nest and thus interested in her. If he is all thumbs and cannot repair a leaky faucet, he may be at a disadvantage at this point. But any man can mow a lawn, which is also related to nest building, or rake leaves, or help move the furniture, or at least take an interest in her daily activities. Maybe you feel that you couldn't care less about the details she relates, but you are expressing love by the very act of listening and thus reinforcing her sense of security.

Some women and men have what could be called the "pack rat syndrome." They like to save string, or magazines, or have little caches of money for some special event. If your wife derives a sense of security from having a checking or savings account of her own, go along with it. It may not make sense to you, but this is not as important as her sense of security. It need not be logical. *Don't try to run your marriage on a steady diet of logic. Feelings are just as important as logic, often more so.* Whatever gives your wife a feeling of security needs to be encouraged as long as it does not disrupt the budget or rob you of your masculine identity.

VIII. Recognize the Validity of Her Moods

All humans vary in their mood swings. Women, however, tend to have somewhat stronger mood variations than most men. Part of this can be attributed to the monthly cycle. With this a husband must learn to be patient and considerate. A woman can appear to be illogical and utterly irrational at times, at least to the male mind that wants things tidy and logical. You may as well accept her variations in mood as inevitable.

Some happy event can make a woman ec-statically happy, or something that has been said or done may plunge her into depression. A rigid or insecure husband can feel threatened by these up and down mood swings. You may prefer a steady pace with no fluctuations, sacrificing the euphoria if you can avoid the depression. Your wife may be constituted differently. Perhaps you married her because of her capacity for joyousness. But a joyous personality can sometimes experience deep depression. You need not ride up to the heights of her happiness if you are wired up differently, nor plunge into her depression. Perhaps one reason she married you was that unconsciously she desired your emotional stability. Don't be panicked or disturbed by mood swings. Ride them out with patience and kindly indulgence. *Don't take it personally* or tell her to "Snap out of it."

IX. Cooperate With Her in Every Effort to Improve Your Marriage

As we have seen, women are insatiable, and men are obtuse. Women can be insatiable in their desire to make a better marriage. Your wife may want you to read a book on marriage or communication or child rearing. Your male ego, if it is a bit weak, may reject this suggested reading, believing there is an implied criticism in her handing you the book to read.

Read it! What do you have to lose? You may even learn something. No one is automatically equipped by a marriage ceremony to function at maximum effectiveness in marriage. Any husband could read a dozen or two books on marriage and profit from the experience.

If she encourages you to visit a marriage counselor with her, or join a group, or go to a series of lectures on marriage or child rearing, by all means go. Marriage and the home involve an all-out activity for a typical woman. Don't be dismayed because she is always pushing for a better relationship. Go along with her graciously and good-naturedly. A marriage counselor can cost a great deal less than a divorce and years and years of child support, besides saving a marriage and avoiding the tears and pain of divorce.

X. Discover Her Particular, Individual Needs and Try to Meet Them

No two wives are alike. The one you married is different from any other woman. She has her own particular set of likes and dislikes, moods, and emotional needs. Her needs may seem limitless at first, or unreasonable. Perhaps you cannot meet all her needs at once, maybe never. But you can try to discover what she needs, wants, and appreciates; you can seek to meet those needs within your capacity. This does not mean catering to childish whims, but it can mean going along with something that may seem illogical or unimportant to you. If it makes her happy and gives her a sense of satisfaction, try to satisfy the need.